PATTERNS OF LIFE

Caring for Young

Caring
for Young

Daphne Butler

RSVP
RAINTREE
STECK-VAUGHN
PUBLISHERS
The Steck-Vaughn Company

Austin, Texas

Published by Raintree Steck-Vaughn Publishers,
an imprint of Steck-Vaughn Company

Design: SPL Design

Library of Congress Cataloging-in-Publication Data

Butler, Daphne. 1945–
    Caring for young / Daphne Butler
        p.   cm.   --   (Patterns of Life)
    Includes index.
    Summary: Describes how animals and humans care for their
offspring, and the role that instinct plays.
    ISBN 0-8172-4201-5
    1. Parental behavior in animals--Juvenile literature. [1. Parental
behavior in animals.] I. Title. II. Series: Butler, Daphne, 1945–
Patterns of life.
QL762.B87   1996
591.56--dc20
                                                                    95-8811
                                                                    CIP
                                                                    AC

Printed and bound in Singapore
by KHL Printing Co Pte Ltd
1 2 3 4 5 6 7 8 9 0   99 98 97 96 95

Photographs: Zefa except for
NHPA (12t, 12br, 14, 15, 17, 19, 21, 22, 24, 27, 29)
Robert Harding (cover, title page)

Contents

When you are very young, someone cares for you all the time.

It might be your mom or your dad or your grandmother. It might be some other grown-up person.

Who takes care of you?

6

Learning Fast

Each day that passes you learn something new. You learn from the people around you.

You also learn from books and television, and by playing.

8

Who Depends on You?

Think about all the people who care for you. They are your family and your friends. Do you care for them, too?

Do you have pets? In what ways do your pets depend on you?

11

Caring in the Wild

Each species has its own way of caring for its young. They do this until the young have grown up.

Mammals are a group of species that feed their babies on milk from their own bodies. The mother and baby stay together for a long time.

Mammals often live together in family groups, or herds, so the young are protected from harm.

Learning to Survive

Young animals learn from their parents. They also learn by playing with other young animals.

They learn how to find food and water. They also learn their place in the family group.

Birds care for their young in a different way from mammals. They find special places to lay their eggs. Some build cozy nests.

The parents take turns sitting on the eggs. They keep them warm until they hatch. Then they work hard to find food for their young brood.

Growing Feathers

Baby birds stay in the nest till their feathers have grown. Then they can learn how to fly. Waterbirds first learn how to paddle.

Many young animals are born in spring. This way they grow strong while there is plenty of food. The weather is warm in spring.

By the time autumn comes, young birds will be fully grown.

Bees are insects. They build nests full of six-sided cells. The queen bee lays an egg in each cell. This egg will hatch as a grub called a larva.

Worker bees feed the larva, which grows big and fat. Then they seal the larva in its cell.

Slowly the larva changes. When it breaks out of its cell, it is a fully grown bee. This change in form is called metamorphosis.

20

Spawn in Spring

Some species never know their children. Frogs leave their spawn, or eggs, in ponds or quiet pools.

The spawn has many lumps of jelly, each with a black speck in the middle. The specks grow, and soon tadpoles hatch.

After some weeks, the tadpoles grow legs, then lungs. Finally, as fully grown frogs, they leave the water for the land.

23

Moths and Butterflies

Moths and butterflies lay their eggs on plants. These plants will make good food for their caterpillars when they hatch.

A caterpillar eats and eats, and finally spins a cocoon.

Inside the cocoon it slowly changes into a moth or butterfly like its parents. When it is fully grown, it breaks out of the cocoon and flies away.

Acting on Instinct

Baby turtles never know their parents. Instinct tells them to leave their nest in the sand. Then, they head for the ocean where they will be safe.

For many animals instinct is the only way of knowing what to do.

People learn a great deal from each other, but they also sometimes know what to do without being told. We cal this acting on instinct. Has it ever happened to you?

amphibians Cold-blooded animals with a smooth skin. These animals live both on land and in the water. Frogs are amphibians.

birds Warm-blooded animals that lay eggs and have feathers on their bodies.

fish Cold-blooded animals that live in water. These animals have scales on their bodies and breathe through gills.

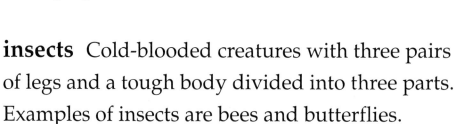

insects Cold-blooded creatures with three pairs of legs and a tough body divided into three parts. Examples of insects are bees and butterflies.

mammals Warm-blooded animals that feed their young on milk from their own bodies. Cows and humans are mammals.

metamorphosis
In this process the body changes its form. Some animals change their form at different stages. The change from caterpillar to butterfly is an example.

species A group of animals, or plants, that are of the same kind and appearance—for example, dogs are a species.

29

Index

Ll
larva 20
learning 8, 15, 18
lungs 23

Mm
mammals 13, 16, 29
metamorphosis 20, 29
moths 25

Nn
nests 16, 20, 26

Pp
parents 15, 16, 25

people 6, 8, 11, 26
pets 11
playing 8, 15

Ss
spawn 23
species 13, 23, 29
spring 18, 23

Tt
tadpoles 23
turtles 26

Ww
water 15, 23, 28
waterbirds 18

31